Native Americans

The Maidu

Barbara A. Gray-Kanatiiosh

ABDO Publishing Company

visit us at
www.abdopublishing.com

Published by ABDO Publishing Company, 8000 West 78th Street, Edina, Minnesota 55439. Copyright © 2002 by Abdo Consulting Group, Inc. International copyrights reserved in all countries. No part of this book may be reproduced in any form without written permission from the publisher.

Printed in the United States of America, North Mankato, Minnesota.
012002   012011

Illustrations: David Kanietakeron Fadden
Interior Photos: Corbis
Editors: Bob Italia, Tamara L. Britton, Kate A. Conley, Kristin Van Cleaf
Art Direction & Maps: Neil Klinepier

Library of Congress Cataloging-in-Publication Data

Gray-Kanatiiosh, Barbara A., 1963-
  The Maidu / Barbara A. Gray-Kanatiiosh
    p. cm. -- (Native Americans)
  Includes index.
  Summary: Presents a brief introduction to the Maidu Indians, including information on their homes, society, food, clothing, family life, and life today.
  ISBN 1-57765-602-4
  1. Maidu Indians--History--Juvenile literature. 2. Maidu Indians--Social life and customs--Juvenile literature. [1. Maidu Indians. 2. Indians of North America--California.] I. Title. II. Native Americans (Edina, Minn.)

E99.M18 G73 2002
979. 4'0049741--dc21

2001046149

About the Author: Barbara A. Gray-Kanatiiosh, JD

Barbara Gray-Kanatiiosh, JD, is an Akwesasne Mohawk. She has a Juris Doctorate from Arizona State University, where she was one of the first recipients of ASU's special certificate in Indian Law. She is currently pursuing a Ph.D. in Justice Studies at ASU and is focusing on Native American issues. Barbara works hard to educate children about Native Americans through her writing and Web site where children may ask questions and receive a written response about the Haudenosaunee culture. The Web site is: www.peace4turtleisland.org

Illustrator: David Kanietakeron Fadden

David Kanietakeron Fadden is a member of the Akwesasne Mohawk Wolf Clan. His work has appeared in publications such as *Akwesasne Notes*, *Indian Time*, and the *Northeast Indian Quarterly*. Examples of his work have appeared in various publications of the Six Nations Indian Museum in Onchiota, NY. His work has also appeared in "How The West Was Lost: Always The Enemy," produced by Gannett Production which appeared on the Discovery Channel. David's work has been exhibited in Albany, NY; the Lake Placid Center for the Arts; Centre Strathearn in Montreal, Quebec; North Country Community College in Saranac Lake, NY; Paul Smith's College in Paul Smiths, NY; and at the Unison Arts & Learning Center in New Paltz, NY.

Contents

Where They Lived 4
Society 6
Food 8
Homes 10
Clothing 12
Crafts 14
Family 16
Children 18
Myths 20
War 22
Contact with Europeans 24
Frank Day 26
The Maidu Today 28
Glossary 30
Web Sites 31
Index 32

Where They Lived

The Maidu (MY-doo) people lived in north central California. They lived in the area bordered by the Sierra Nevada mountains, and the Sacramento, Feather, and American Rivers. The Maidu lands had mountains, steep hills, valleys, forests, meadows, rivers, and lakes.

There were three groups of Maidu. They were the Mountain Maidu, the Northwestern Maidu, and the Southern Maidu. Each group had their own traditional homeland and language.

The Mountain Maidu lived in the Sierra Nevada mountains. They spoke the language Maidu. The Northwestern Maidu lived in the mountain foothills. They spoke Konkow (CON-cow). The Southern Maidu lived in the valleys. They spoke Nisenan (NEESAH-non).

The Sierra Nevada foothills

The Maidu Homelands

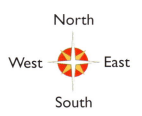

DETAIL AREA

5

Society

The Maidu lived in village communities. All the people in a village community shared the land. About 200 people lived in each community. These communities were usually located along a river.

Each community had three to five villages. One of these was the main village. It contained the ceremonial roundhouse. It was also home to the village chief.

The chief spoke for and advised the people. He led his people into battle, but also worked to keep peace. He organized hunting, fishing, **raiding**, and ceremonial activities, too.

Pairs of men guarded their village's borders. These men wore **magpie** feathers on their heads. The men were chosen for this important job for their good judgement and even tempers.

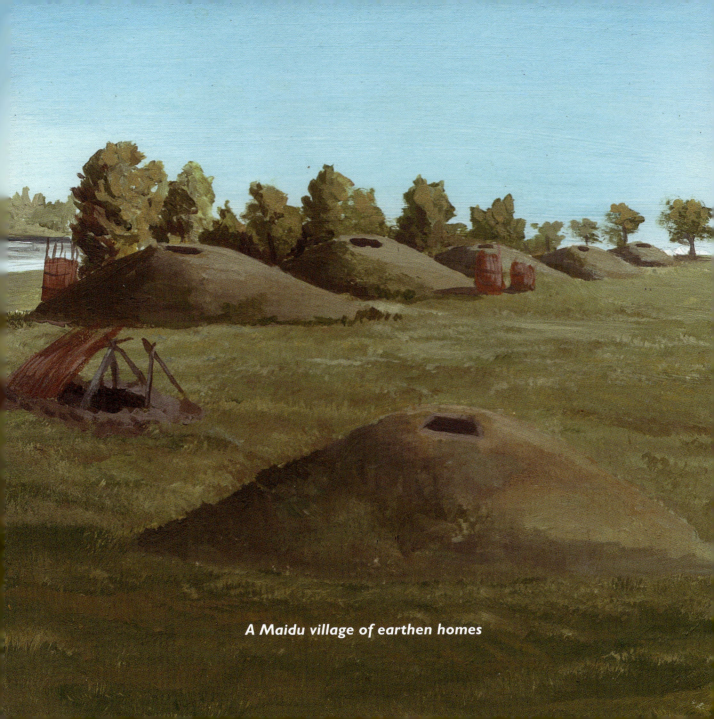
A Maidu village of earthen homes

Food

    The Maidu hunted using bows and arrows, spears, and knives. They made knife blades and spearheads from **basalt** and **obsidian**. The Maidu hunted pronghorn, deer, elk, squirrels, rabbits, ducks, geese, and quail.

    The Maidu caught fish with hooks they carved from bone. They also used nets and baskets to trap fish. They fished for salmon, eel, and other types of fish.

    The Maidu also gathered many types of wild foods. They gathered wild roots, berries, seeds, nuts, and insects. Using a digging stick, they gathered blue camas, cattail, and other roots. They used long sticks to knock hazelnuts, buckeyes, and acorns from the trees.

    The Maidu ate acorns as the main part of their diet. Before they could eat them, they had to remove the acorns' bitter taste. To do this, the Maidu first shelled the acorns. Then they ground them into **meal**. They poured water over the meal until it washed away the bitterness. The Maidu made the acorn **meal** into soup, mush, and bread.

The Maidu also gathered and ate insects. They ate locusts, grasshoppers, crickets, and yellow-jacket **larva**. They roasted them in baskets with hot coals.

A Maidu fisherman uses a net to catch fish.

Homes

    The Maidu built different kinds of homes depending on the seasons. In the winter, the Mountain Maidu lived in bark-covered houses. To build a bark home, the Maidu made a circular frame of upright poles. Then they harvested large slabs of redwood or cedar bark. They tied the bark to the frame. They covered the door with animal fur.

    The Maidu who lived at the foot of the mountains lived in earthen homes. To build an earth-covered home, the Maidu first dug a hole in the ground. Then they built a wooden frame over the hole. They covered the frame with woven **tule** (TOO-lee) mats or grass. Then they packed earth on top of the mats.

    The Maidu moved often during the summer and gathering seasons. At these times, they lived in temporary **brush** shelters. They made these homes by standing four poles upright in the ground. The poles supported a flat roof made from tree branches and leaves.

The Maidu also built village community roundhouses. The roundhouses held many people for ceremonies and meetings.

To build a roundhouse, the Maidu dug a pit 4 feet (1.2 m) deep and 10 to 15 feet (3 to 5 m) wide. Then they placed four large wooden poles upright in the center of the pit. They tied **brush**, **tule**, and earth on the frame to create the walls and roof.

Earthen home

Bark-covered home

Brush shelter

Clothing

In the summer, the Maidu wore few pieces of clothing. The men wore **breechcloths** made from **buckskin** or wire grass. The women wore aprons. They made the aprons from buckskin and plants such as grass, willow, and shredded bark. Both men and women wore deerskin moccasins.

In the winter, the Maidu wore more clothing to keep warm. They wore deerskin **leggings** with the fur turned toward their legs. They also wore fur robes and woven duck or goose feather blankets. The Maidu stuffed their moccasins with grass to keep their feet warm.

The women wore basket hats woven with **geometric** designs. During ceremonies, men wore hair nets woven from plant fibers. They also wore feathered belts and headbands.

Both men and women usually had long hair. If they cut their hair, they used hot coals. They wore bone, shell, feather, and wood jewelry.

For ceremonies, the Maidu painted their bodies with paint they made from white or red clay, red stone, or charcoal. They also **tattooed** their upper bodies. To do this, they used a sharp fish or bird bone to make designs of lines and dots on their skin. Then they rubbed paint into the cuts.

A Maidu family in traditional clothing

Crafts

    The Maidu were skilled craftspeople. Maidu men made rafts and canoes. They made rafts by tying logs together with plant fiber ropes.

    The Maidu made dugout, plank, and reed canoes. They made dugout canoes from large, straight trees. First, they cut the trees down using stone axes and fire. They removed the tree's bark with a stone. Then they hollowed out the log with fire.

    To make plank canoes, the Maidu collected tree bark. Then they wove the bark into planks. They also gathered **tule** reeds into bundles to make reed canoes.

    The Maidu were excellent weavers. Maidu craftspeople wove nets to catch fish and birds. To make a net, they rolled milkweed plant fibers into string. They wove the string into nets.

    The weavers also wove coiled and **twined** baskets. They used plants such as redbud, willow, bear grass, yellow pine, and ferns to weave baskets.

The Maidu used the **twining** method to make seed beater baskets, fish traps, and women's cone-shaped hats. They also made **watertight** coiled baskets. The Maidu used them for cooking, storage, and ceremonies.

Maidu weavers also wove ceremonial baskets using plant materials and woodpecker and quail feathers. Sometimes they decorated the baskets with shell beads.

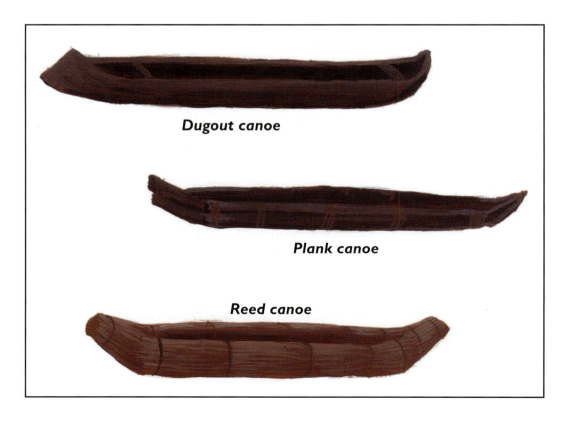

Dugout canoe

Plank canoe

Reed canoe

Family

Maidu men and women were free to choose their marriage partner. But their families had to agree on their choice.

When a Maidu couple decided to get married, the man gave gifts to the woman's family. He gave meat to show that he was a good provider. He also gave shells and beads.

If the woman's family accepted the gifts, the man moved into the woman's village. He stayed in the village and provided for the woman and her family. After about six months, the couple was considered married. Then they moved to the man's village.

Each person in a Maidu family had a family responsibility. Men hunted and fished. They made tools such as axes, bows, and arrows. They also wove fishing nets and fishing traps.

Women gathered food to cook and prepare for storage. They made clothing and wove baskets. They cared for their children. Elder men and women also helped raise the children.

When a family member died, the Maidu burned all of the person's possessions. This **memorial** burning helped the Maidu to deal with the loss of their loved one.

Maidu women gathering food and cooking a meal

Children

Maidu women carried their babies in **tule** cradle baskets. Maidu **ritual** required that the first cradle basket be used for two weeks and then thrown away. Then the Maidu made a new cradle basket. The baby used the second cradle until he or she started walking.

The Maidu did not name their babies until they were two or three years old. Sometimes a baby was named in honor of an ancestor. Other times, people watched the baby and gave the child a name that fitted her or his personality.

Children learned from their families. Women taught girls how to make baskets and prepare food. The girls learned how to make acorn bread, soup, and mush. Men taught boys how to hunt and weave fish traps and other items.

Children also learned by helping their parents and elders. They chased rabbits and quail into nets during a hunt. They also helped to gather acorns, seeds, and roots.

Boys and girls also played many types of games. Some made their minds strong. Other games made their bodies strong. They often had foot races and swimming contests.

A Maidu mother holds her baby in a tule cradle basket.

Myths

The following is a Maidu story of creation. It tells how the Creator made the land and its people.

Long ago, Turtle sat on a raft. He was floating on endless water. Suddenly, a bright light shone from the sky. It was the Creator. The Creator traveled through the sky and sat on the raft next to Turtle.

Turtle said, "I wish there was some land." The Creator said, "Dive down to the bottom of the water. Get me some mud and I will make land." Turtle said, "I can only dive so far. Then I float back to the top." So the Creator tied a rock to Turtle's arm to help him dive.

Turtle dove into the water. He stayed under the water for six years. When he came back up, he had mud in his claws.

The Creator took the mud and rolled it into a ball. He placed the ball on the raft. The ball of mud grew and grew until it became the Earth.

Then the Creator made the stars, oak trees, birds, and many kinds of animals. He also made man and woman.

Turtle sitting on a raft

War

    The Maidu tried to keep peace with other tribes. When the tribes and village communities were at peace, they could trade with each other. They traded for things such as pine nuts, **obsidian**, and abalone and disk shells.

    But sometimes another tribe entered the Maidu's hunting, gathering, or fishing territory without permission. The Maidu would then go to war to protect their lands. The Maidu used spears, knives, slings, and bows and arrows as weapons. Sometimes they dipped their arrows in poison.

    Armor protected the men from injury. Men wore two kinds of armor. One type was elk **hide** worn from their knees up to their shoulders. They also wore armor made from mahogany sticks tied together to form mats. The men wrapped the mats around their bodies. The mats reached up to their chins. If an arrow was coming toward a man's head, he could tuck his head down behind the mahogany mat.

When fighting, Maidu men faced the enemy with the sides of their bodies. This exposed less of their bodies and made it harder for the enemy to hit them.

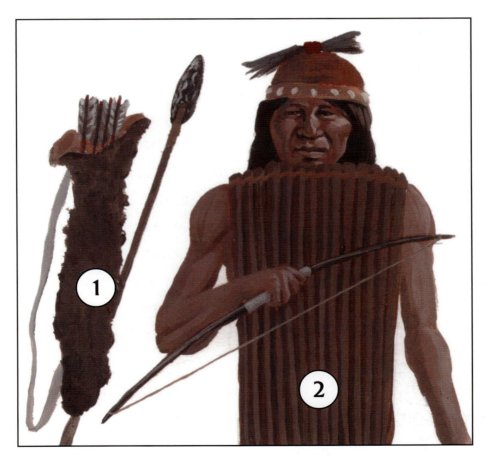

1. Arrows in a quiver, and a spear. 2. A Maidu warrior wearing a protective mat and holding a bow.

Contact with Europeans

In 1808, Spanish explorer Gabriel Moraga explored Maidu lands. In the 1820s and 1830s, fur trappers moved into California. Trappers from the American Fur Company and Hudson's Bay Company gathered beaver **pelts**.

For a time, the Maidu and the trappers shared the land. But the trappers brought many diseases that the Maidu did not have natural defenses against. In 1833, a Malaria **epidemic** killed many Maidu people. Entire villages died.

In 1849, miners discovered gold in Maidu territory. The California Gold Rush began. Soon gold miners came by the thousands. This sudden increase in population harmed the Maidu and their way of life. The miners brought pigs, cows, and other livestock. The livestock grazed on the Maidu lands. The plants and animals the Maidu depended on for food became harder to find. Some Maidu starved. Others were killed by miners and settlers.

In 1863, U.S. soldiers came to the Maidu homelands. The soldiers forced the Maidu from their lands. The Maidu marched for two weeks until they arrived at the Round Valley **Reservation** in Covelo, California. In the 1950s, the U.S. government's policy of **termination** ended official recognition of many tribes. The Maidu lost their remaining lands and federal funding.

A Maidu man encounters a fur trapper.

Frank Day

Frank Day was born in 1902, in Berry Creek, California. His father, Billy Day, was one of the last traditional chiefs of his village.

As a young man, Frank Day learned the traditional teachings of his people. Maidu elders taught him the songs, dances, and stories of the Maidu **culture**. Day spoke his native language of Konkow.

In the 1960s, Day became an artist. Some of his paintings show spirits and characters from legends. Other paintings show ceremonial burnings. His artwork shows people Maidu stories and culture.

Frank Day died in 1976. But through his artwork, he left future generations a visual record of the Maidu's vanishing culture.

Frank Day

 # The Maidu Today

Today, there are about 3,550 Maidu. Many have become artists, teachers, or doctors. Maidu live all over the world. But many still live on **rancherias** in California. The Berry Creek, Enterprise, Greenville, and Mooretown Rancherias of Maidu Indians are federally recognized tribes.

But many Maidu have no land. They are fighting legal battles to regain their traditional homelands. They want to be recognized as tribes by the federal government.

The Maidu are working to restore and strengthen their **culture**. They are teaching their children the tribe's languages, stories, dances, and songs. They are building houses and restoring their lands. Some Maidu tribes are funding these efforts with money made from casinos.

Spring flowers carpet the grassy slopes of the Sierra Nevada foothills, part of the Maidu traditional homelands.

The Sierra Nevada mountains

Glossary

basalt - a dense, dark gray or black rock.
breechcloth - a piece of hide or cloth wrapped between the legs and tied with a belt around the waist.
brush - cut or broken twigs or branches.
buckskin - a soft, bendable leather.
culture - the customs, arts, and tools of a nation or people at a certain time.
epidemic - the rapid spread of a disease among many people at the same time.
geometric - made up of straight lines, circles, and other simple shapes.
hide - an animal skin that is often thick and heavy.
larva - a newly-hatched, wormlike insect.
leggings - a covering for the leg, usually made of leather or cloth.
magpie - a noisy, long-tailed black bird that has a stout, black and white bill.
meal - coarsely ground seed.
memorial - something that serves as a remembrance of a person or an event.
obsidian - a hard, glassy rock formed when molten lava cools.
pelt - an animal skin with the fur still on it.
raid - a surprise attack by a small force.

rancheria - a Native American village.

reservation - a piece of land set aside by the U.S. government for Native Americans to live on.

ritual - a system of ceremonial acts or actions.

tattoo - to permanently mark the skin with figures or designs.

termination - to bring to an end.

tule - a type of reed that grows in wetlands. Tule is native to California.

twine - to form by twisting, interweaving, or interlacing.

watertight - made so that no water can pass in or out.

Web Sites

Frank Day
http://www.conexus.si.edu/day/index.htm
Learn more about Frank Day and his work at this site from the National Museum of the American Indian.

The ConCow Maidu
http://www.maidu.com
Learn about the Konkow Valley Band of ConCow Maidu.

These sites are subject to change. Go to your favorite search engine and type in Maidu for more sites.

Index

A

art 26

C

California Gold Rush 24
canoes 14
casinos 28
ceremonies 6, 11, 12, 13, 15, 26
chiefs 6, 26
children 16, 18, 19
clothing 6, 12, 16
cradle baskets 18
crafts 14, 15, 18, 26

D

dances 26, 28
Day, Frank 26
death 17, 24
disease 24

F

family 16, 17, 18
fishing 6, 8, 16
food 8, 9, 16, 18, 24

G

games 19
gathering 8, 9, 16, 18, 24

H

homelands 4, 10, 24, 25, 28
homes 6, 10, 11, 28
hunting 6, 8, 16, 18

L

language 4, 26, 28

M

marriage 16
Moraga, Gabriel 24

R

raiding 6
rancherias 28
reservations 25
roundhouse 6, 11

S

settlers (American) 24
society 6

songs 26, 28
Spanish 24
stories 20, 21, 26, 28

T

tattoos 13
tools 8, 14, 15, 16, 18
trade 22
tribes 4, 22, 25, 28

U

U.S. government 25, 28
U.S. soldiers 25

V

villages 6, 11, 16, 22, 24

W

war 6, 22, 23
weapons 8, 16, 22, 23